THat's WHat's DiFFeReNt ABoUT Me!

M.E.I. ELEMENTARY
LIBRARY

MEI Elementary School
31655 Downes Rd.
Abbotsford, B.C   V4X 2M8

More Enthusiastic Reviews of
That's What's Different About Me!

"Heather McCracken has created a marvelous teaching tool to assist educators in fostering mutual friendships between children with autism and their classmates. The combination of a clear and comprehensive manual, a fun and friendly training DVD and a delightfully illustrated coloring and story book makes for a complete and ease-to-use package."

— Kari Dunn Buron, autism resource specialist, author of *When My Autism Gets Too Big!* and co-author of *The Incredible 5-Point Scale*

"As a parent of two children with autism, I know how important it is that other children learn to understand autism. *That's What's Different About Me!* helps make that happen. Not only do the children see my son in the puppets, but sometimes they see themselves and have something to relate to. The puppets are amazing at opening the door to understanding, inclusion and acceptance."

— Cynthia Gerlach, parent

"*That's What's Different About Me!* is an innovative program that helps young children to understand and accept differences in peers with autism spectrum disorders. Children will immediately begin using the friendship skills depicted during the captivating puppet show on the DVD."

— Sue Rampone, speech-language pathologist, Central Okanagan School District, Kelowna, Canada

"I have found the *That's What's Different About Me!* program by Heather McCracken to be an invaluable teaching tool and resource for both students and teachers. The puppet presentation captivates students who learn best through both visual and auditory modalities and provides important concepts about how to build friendships with children on the autism spectrum. Kudos to the creators for developing an autism demystification program that is heartwarming, sensitive, user-friendly, and unique."

— Elizabeth Rich, BCABA, consultant and special education teacher, Fredonia Central Schools, Fredonia, New York

"Heather McCracken and the Friend 2 Friend Social Learning Society have delighted thousands of school children with their unique approach to learning about their classmates with autism spectrum disorders. This delightful resource continues this work, making it accessible to an even greater audience. It is extremely practical for educators, using empirically sound strategies, and is all the more valuable because of the work of dedicated parents who understand the need for children with ASD to be accepted by their classmates."

— Laurie Smith, principal, School District #42, Maple Ridge-Pitt Meadows, British Columbia, Canada

THAT'S WHAT'S DIFFERENT ABOUT ME!

Helping Children Understand Autism Spectrum Disorders

Program Manual

Heather McCracken

Foreword by Pamela Wolfberg, Ph.D.

Autism Asperger Publishing Co.
P.O. Box 23173
Shawnee Mission, Kansas 66283-0173
www.asperger.net

© 2006 Autism Asperger Publishing Co.
P.O. Box 23173
Shawnee Mission, Kansas 66283-0173
www.asperger.net

All rights reserved. No part of the material protected by this copyright notice may be reproduced or used in any form or by any means, electronic or mechanical, including photocopying, recording, or by any information storage and retrieval system, without the prior written permission of the copyright owner.

ISBN: 1-931282-96-X

This book is designed in Helvetica Neue, Highlander and Hot Coffee.

Printed in the United States of America.

Dedication

I would like to dedicate this program to my father, the late William Richard McCracken (Dick), 1934-1976, the first person to teach me the importance of understanding, acceptance and empathy.

To my three remarkable children, Katie, Iain and Emma, their understanding, acceptance, empathy and friendship for one another is my model for life.

And to my wonderful husband, Dave, who has supported the development of these programs with his unconditional acceptance, understanding, empathy, friendship and love.

This song is for you,
Heather McCracken (Mom)

Acknowledgments

Many people have supported the development and delivery of the Friend 2 Friend programs throughout the years. I would like to thank the following, without whose support the Friend 2 Friend programs would not be possible.

To the Friend 2 Friend presenting team, who works tirelessly to bring the Friend 2 Friend programs to children throughout British Columbia:
Janet Cregan, Monique Hoekstra, Joanne McCartney, Leanna Mills, Tricia Pederson, Diane Tucker, Tanya Vipond. And to Linda Chamrad – Connecticut, United States; Shareen Evans – Quesnel, BC; and Coral Loader – Australia.

To the Friend 2 Friend Board of Directors:
Paul Bowes, Joanne Brennan, Ken Brown, Monique Hoekstra, Wendy Holtan and David Robbins.

To Judi Langley, who inspired me to say "What do you need?" and then find a way to provide it. And to Marjanne, Michelle, Margie, Andrea and Marion who taught me how.

To my mentor and dear friend, Pamela Wolfberg, the person I turn to the most for advice, support and sometimes just a good laugh.

And to the many parents, teachers, principals, speech and language pathologists and other professionals who have welcomed the Friend 2 Friend programs into their schools and homes.

Most important, to the thousands of children on the autism spectrum and their peers, for teaching me a new lesson every day!

Table of Contents

Foreword 1

Preface 3

Introduction 5

Section One – Friend 2 Friend Philosophy 7

    The Importance of Friendships 7

    The Social Void 8

    Addressing the Social Void – Autism Demystification 10

Section Two – Friend 2 Friend Teaching Model 11

    Fostering Mutual Friendships by Modeling, Labeling, Explaining and Normalizing 11

    Friend 2 Friend Learning Goals 12

        • Five Key Learning Goals 13

    Prosocial Communication Strategies 13

        • Seven Basic Friendship Tips 14

Section Three – *That's What's Different About Me!* Puppet Program 15

    Program Overview 15

    Supporting the Focus Child's Participation 18

    Implementing the Program 19

        • Lesson Plan 1 – The Puppet Play 20

        • Lesson Plan 2 – Children's Story and Coloring Book 21

        • Lesson Plan 3 – Puppet Role-Playing 22

    Follow-Up Activities and Resources 24

    Friend 2 Friend Materials 29

Section Four – Regular and Continuous Support 32

    The Integrated Play Groups Model by Dr. Pamela Wolfberg 32

    References 37

FOREWORD

When I think back to my closest friendships in childhood, I recall with great clarity the intensity of the experiences and depth of feelings we shared. Even after many decades (more than I care to admit), the images and sensations associated with my earliest friendships remain vivid. I can still remember the feeling of 'butterflies in my stomach' when I knocked on the door of our new neighbor to meet the girl who became my instant playmate and best friend. Our friendship bond was sealed as we discovered our mutual passion for make-believe play, musical performances and delectable treats. It was as if time stood still and adults ceased to exist while we were deeply immersed in the social and imaginary worlds we created together.

> *I remember as a little girl playing runaway orphans with my two sisters and neighborhood friend. We were quite fond of the popular tales* Peter Pan *and* Oliver Twist. *We gathered together all of our dolls and stuffed animals in blankets. My one sister brought along Mr. Peabody, her imaginary friend. Together we went out to explore the "never-never-land" of all the backyards in the neighborhood. Every step of the way we encountered a new adventure – imagining near escapes from evil foes, seeking refuge in forts of leaves and snow.* (Wolfberg, 1999, p. 23)

Although proximity was clearly a factor in the formation of my early friendship with my neighbor, our friendship circle expanded as we entered school together. It wasn't long before we embraced a new best friend, who has remained a trusted friend. As friends growing up together, our friendship bond gradually took on new meaning. We not only sought each other out for fun, but also for intimacy, support and solace. The dynamics of our friendship were not without complications. We had our share of conflicts, disputes and painful moments, enduring feelings of anger, sadness and jealousy. In the early years, the terrain was ripe with quarrels over coveted possessions and vying for each other's undivided attention. As we grew closer to adolescence, the stakes became higher, with mounting tension over social status in cliques and loyalty to friends over boyfriends. Nevertheless, it is these friendship experiences – the good, the bad and the ugly – that are essentially life's social lessons that prepare us for adulthood.

Friendship is a most powerful, meaningful and essential part of human existence. Friends occupy a central place in our social lives over our lifespan. I am acutely aware of how very privileged I am to be able to reflect on my most valued friendships – past friends who have come and gone, friends today who have stood the test of time, and friends (including Heather McCracken) who have recently entered my life – all of whom I cherish in distinct ways. The thought of never having had any one of these friendships leaves me cold and empty – as if there were a huge void at the very center of my being.

As Heather McCracken poignantly describes, she created the Friend 2 Friend model out of necessity for her son, who at the time did not have any friends. The fact that her son was diagnosed with an autism spectrum disorder placed him at a clear disadvantage for relating to other children in the same way as typically developing children relate to one another. Autism is a complex neurobiological disorder characterized by impaired social interactions, problems with verbal and non-verbal communication, and unusual, repetitive, or limited activities or interests. In light of these inherent issues, children with autism face significant challenges forming social relationships, and particularly friendships.

As Heather also aptly points out, children with autism are no different than other children in their desire for peer acceptance and companionship. What differs is that they express social overtures in ways that are uniquely their own. The idiosyncratic ways in which they may attempt to socially engage peers is likely to backfire if the peers have no framework for understanding the child with autism. Without any form of preparation, typical peers are unlikely to react positively to children who behave in unexpected ways. Consequently, children with autism often fall victims to teasing and rejection or are overlooked and neglected by peers. Without a system of support, they are especially vulnerable to being excluded from their peer culture, and thus deprived of opportunities to actualize their potential to socialize and make friends. Further, without the benefit of friendships, they are at high risk for continued social difficulties that may be compounded in later life.

The Friend 2 Friend model is designed as a first step toward breaking this vicious cycle by helping children understand and be a friend to someone who has an autism spectrum disorder. This groundbreaking work is possibly one of the most important contributions to the field today – a field that has expanded exponentially in recent years in an effort to respond to a growing population that has reached epidemic proportions. While an outpouring of publications have focused on a wide variety of methods to address the unique needs of children with autism, there is a relative dearth of materials devoted to helping children develop friendships. The Friend 2 Friend model's state-of-the-art puppet and related programs fill this void.

The Friend 2 Friend model has already reached countless children across North America, and will undoubtedly reach countless more as professionals and families apply the practices in school, home and community settings. Friend 2 Friend has become an essential component of my own practice, which involves developing inclusive peer play programs via the Integrated Play Groups model. It is a profound privilege to know Heather not only because Friend 2 Friend is such an innovative model, but because of our friendship that has emerged out of our shared passion and value for bringing children together for play and friendship.

Pamela Wolfberg, Ph.D.
San Francisco State University & Autism Institute on Peer Relations and Play

Preface

I stood outside the classroom peeking in, powerless to enter because I didn't want my son's third-grade teacher to think I was "interfering." I just stood there, helplessly watching my son fall apart. I took action only when I saw the teacher wave his arm toward the door and say "GET OUT." It was like watching my son falling down the rabbit hole, knowing there was nothing I could do to stop his descent into panic and despair. As soon as he appeared, I approached him and said "it is okay" as I sat down on the floor beside him to help him calm down.

Some time later I learned that the reason why my son had become so distressed that day was that he had brought his favorite video in hopes of "sharing" it with his classmates. He had asked his teacher when he arrived that morning if he could "tell" the class about the video. The teacher said yes and told him that he could do it at three o'clock. Three o'clock came, and when my son took his place at the front of the classroom to share his video with his classmates, the children packed up and left. My son was devastated. This was the third day of third grade. Needless to say, this was not a good start to the new school year.

Over the next three months my son's ability to cope with the expectations at school continued to deteriorate, and by early December it was clear that we needed to remove him from his home school. Once we made that decision, I was overcome with a sense of relief but felt physically ill at the same time. It would be some time before I could accept the fact that there was no one who could fix the issues facing my son at school. There was no program, no expert, no one to help support the one thing that my son desired above everything else – friends.

Watching my son suffer from social isolation at school, I felt compelled to do whatever I could to help him and other children who experience social and emotional rejection within their peer group. Over the next year while home-schooling my 7-year-old son and 4-year-old daughter, I began researching and developing what are now known as the Friend 2 Friend programs. I wanted to develop fun and interactive programs that would provide children with information about autism in an age-appropriate and sensitive manner. I felt that if my son's peers could learn to understand his unique social communication style in the same way his sisters understand, accept and empathize with their brother, we would move him one step closer to the friendships he desired.

In 2002 my husband and I founded Friend 2 Friend Social Learning Society, a non-profit charity based in North Vancouver, British Columbia, Canada, and began delivering a 10-line puppet play to children in our neighborhood schools and preschools. Over the years that 10-line puppet play has evolved into a comprehensive package of programs for children aged 3-18, as well as training seminars for parents and professionals. To date Friend 2 Friend has visited over 45,000 school-aged children and 20,000 adults throughout British Columbia and the United States.

It is my hope that with the help of Friend 2 Friend programs we can all work proactively to foster understanding, acceptance, empathy and mutual friendships between extraordinary individuals on the autism spectrum and their peers, siblings and classmates.

"Each friend represents a world in us, a world not born until they arrive, and it is only by this meeting that a new world is born."

Anais Nin

INTRODUCTION

The Friend 2 Friend Social Learning Society has one mandate: to foster mutual friendships between children on the autism spectrum and their peers, siblings and classmates. To meet this mandate Friend 2 Friend has developed and delivers autism demystification and educational programs for children aged 3-18 and training seminars for parents and professionals.

Friend 2 Friend's first program, the puppet presentation, is a comprehensive program designed to demystify children aged 3-10 about the characteristics of autism while introducing them to communication strategies that promote successful social interactions between typical peers and children on the autism spectrum.

That's What's Different About Me! is a packaged puppet program designed for self-use by parents, teachers and other professionals. The program provides a step-by-step method for implementing the principles and practices of Friend 2 Friend puppet presentations at school, at home or in therapeutic settings.

That's What's Different About Me! contains:

- ***That's What's Different About Me!* DVD:** This interactive DVD contains (a) a brief introduction for teachers and parents, (b) the puppet play, (c) "What Did Crystal Learn?" [a review of the learning goals and friendship tips introduced in the puppet play] and (d) frequently asked questions. All sections have optional closed-caption translations in the United Nations recognized languages.

- ***That's What's Different About Me!* Program Manual:** This manual is designed to assist in implementing the *That's What's Different About Me!* program at home or at school. The manual introduces readers to the basic concepts, principles, tools and techniques of the Friend 2 Friend teaching model. You will find four main sections. Section One looks at the philosophy of the Friend 2 Friend programs. Section Two introduces the Friend 2 Friend teaching model. Section Three outlines how to implement the program, including lesson plans, follow-up activities, resources and materials. The final section provides an overview of our sister model, the Integrated Play Groups (IPG), written by the creator of the IPG, Dr. Pamela Wolfberg.

- ***That's What's Different About Me! Children's Story and Coloring Book***: This story and coloring book tells the story of Crystal and how she and Freddie learned to be better friends. It is adapted from the Friend 2 Friend puppet play (as seen on the DVD) into a readable story and coloring book for classroom use.

Folkmanis Puppets: Puppets may be purchased through Folkmanis Puppets, www.folkmanis.com

Note. That's What's Different About Me! program manual offers an overview of the Friend 2 Friend principles and practices. To gain a comprehensive understanding of the Friend 2 Friend teaching model, we suggest you participate in the Friend 2 Friend training seminars. For more information on training, please visit our website at www.friend2friendsociety.org or contact our office at friend2friend@shaw.ca

Section One
Friend 2 Friend Philosophy

The Importance of Friendships

All children want friends and to feel accepted within their peer group. Making friends, for children on the autism spectrum, can be a difficult task because they often lack the social skill building blocks needed to achieve their goal. However, their lack of skills should never be confused with a lack of desire. All children, regardless of their unique challenges or gifts, have the intrinsic need to play and make friends. Children with autism are no different – they just express this need differently. (McCracken, 2004)

What does the word friendship mean to you? For each of us the word conjures up memories of childhood play, feelings of joy, sometimes even feelings of loneliness. In childhood, school is the primary natural setting for the development of friendships and play, offering children the opportunity for shared social experiences within their natural peer group. It is in these shared social experiences with peers that children start to form the social skills they need to develop, maintain, and perhaps end, friendships for the rest of their lives.

However, for many children on the autism spectrum these skills do not develop unsupported and are often not the focus of the educational system, leaving these children out of an essential part of the human experience.

Friendships are vitally important to a child's social and emotional development, providing the basis for children to become well-adjusted, caring and productive adults (Hartup, 1989, 1991; Ladd, 1990). Studies show that children with mutual friends are more socially competent and better adjusted than children without friends. Research also suggests that friendships are not only associated with children's social, emotional and cognitive development, but is a determining factor in their social and professional abilities as adults. Specifically, children who have friends tend to have higher self-esteem, are more sociable and cooperative, and better able to cope with change and manage interpersonal conflicts (Berndt, 1999, 2002). It is in friendships that children build the confidence to try new things and experience the world around them. The safety of friendships and the feeling of acceptance by their peers provides *all children* with guidance, companionship, recreation, creativity, emotional support and academic motivation. These pivotal roles make friendships a logical focus when supporting children on the autism spectrum to develop to the best of their abilities through the play and socialization that friendships provide.

It is widely recognized that the shared social experiences and the development of friendships within a natural peer group support children with autism spectrum disorders (ASD) to build skills not otherwise obtained. However, what is often overlooked is that these friendships provide typically developing peers with equally important benefits. The benefits of friendships between children on the autism spectrum and their peers are far reaching for all children (Wolfberg, McCracken, & Tuchel, in press). These benefits include the following:

Benefits for Children With ASD
- Decreased anxiety and stress
- Increased interests and play skills
- Increased communication skills
- Increased self-confidence
- Fun and friendships

Benefits for Peers, Siblings and Classmates
- Sense of pride in helping others
- Better understanding/appreciation of diversity
- Increased self-confidence
- Better communication/leadership skills
- Fun and friendships

The Social Void

Friendships between children on the autism spectrum and their typically developing peers often fail to develop. Frequently, there is a void between children on the autism spectrum and their typically developing peers. This social void begins to surface between the ages of 7 and 9 when children start to make social comparisons (Thompson & Rubin, 2002). That is, at this age children begin to measure their abilities and skills against their peers' abilities and skills. If the child on the autism spectrum exhibits unusual characteristics such as odd or delayed social skills, unusual communication style or self-regulating behaviors, peers notice that the child behaves in a manner that is not "normal" or "typical" compared to peers.

Once peers start to recognize these differences, they need information to understand the differences they see. If we do not supply children with a common conceptual framework and language to understand the differences between themselves and the child on the autism spectrum, the social comparisons often become social judgments. That is, due to a lack of information about autism, children will make judgments based on incorrect assumptions and conjecture.

The social void between children on the autism spectrum and their peers is a direct result of a lack of shared understanding, acceptance and empathy towards the unique characteristics and experiences of individuals on the autism spectrum. When a social void exists, the child on the autism spectrum often remains on the periphery of the peer group, causing him to feel alienated within the school environment, which may lead to feelings of loneliness and depression (Asher, Hymel, & Remshaw, 1984).

Many factors contribute to the social void between children on the autism spectrum and their typical peers, including the following.

Typical Peers ...
- Notice that the child on the autism spectrum behaves in a manner that is different to them (social comparisons)
- Do not have information about autism spectrum disorders and, therefore, are unable to understand the differences they see
- Are reluctant to ask questions or express their feelings regarding the differences between themselves and their peer on the autism spectrum
- Attempt to play with their peer on the autism spectrum but are often unsuccessful because they do not have the appropriate prosocial skills to interact successfully

The Focus Child (Child on the Autism Spectrum) ...
- Notices the differences between him/herself and peers (social comparisons)
- Feels alienated from the peer group because of these differences
- Has little information about autism and, therefore, is unable to understand his or her differences and does not have language to explain those differences
- Has delayed social skills

    Note. Children with autism often attempt to play with their peers but their attempts are awkward or unusual, and peers are not aware that these active, odd or aloof social (Wing, 1981) attempts are the child's only way of initiating play and expressing the desire to make friends.

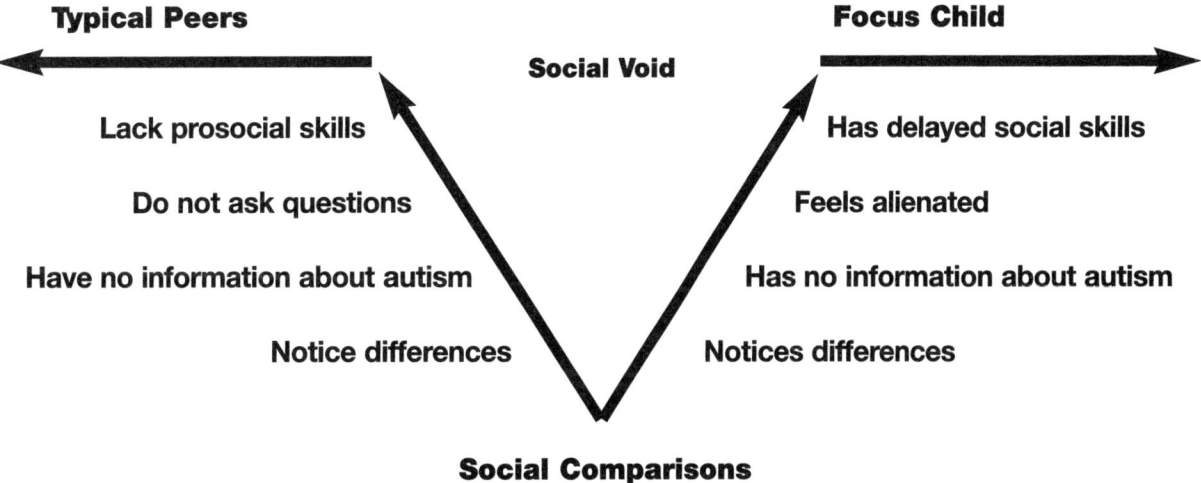

Addressing the Social Void – Autism Demystification

All children need information about autism to help them provide the social supports that are an essential part of educating children on the autism spectrum in an integrated setting. Providing children with information about autism in an age-appropriate and sensitive manner creates a truly inclusive school environment and models a respect for diversity. Autism demystification is central to fostering mutual friendships between children with autism and their peers, siblings and classmates.

Based on a careful analysis of the issues facing children on the autism spectrum in making and keeping friends, Friend 2 Friend has developed a set of guidelines for autism demystification that provides sensitive information about autism in a manner that includes the focus child and models a respect for everyone's affinities (gifts) and challenges (disabilities). Using this guideline is a critical component in the Friend 2 Friend programs.

Friend 2 Friend Autism Demystification Guidelines

- Autism demystification begins by supporting the focus child (child on the autism spectrum) to understand and accept her own unique challenges and gifts. Supporting children with autism to understand and accept their unique kinds of minds models a respect for individuality and diversity.

- Autism demystification programs for peers should include the focus child. This provides the focus child with the opportunity to receive the same information that peers are receiving and models respect for diversity and a truly inclusive classroom or school. *"Not about me without me."*

- Autism demystification should be delivered in a sensitive, age-appropriate, fun and interactive way. For young children, it should be provided in the way that children learn best – through play and imagination. Talking to young children about autism is often not as effective as communicating through games, story books and fun activities.

- Autism demystification should never "single out" the child with autism, nor should the child's name, diagnosis or any personal information be discussed. When presenting sensitive information, confidentiality is critical. *"Autism demystification is not autism identification."*

- Autism demystification should always include examples of other individuals with autism or role-playing to help generalize characteristics of autism, which supports the understanding and acceptance of these characteristics.

- Autism demystification should use sensitive language and encourage a shared vocabulary, such as "I have the kind of mind …," "We are all different in our own way," and "This is my stim, what's yours?"

- Autism demystification should be direct and honest, respecting individuality, diversity and privacy. *"Autism is not a four-letter word."*

By following these simple guidelines, autism demystification programs or activities will support children in understanding, accepting and empathizing with their peers on the autism spectrum. This is the first step in fostering mutual friendships between children with autism and their peers, siblings and classmates (Feshback & Feshback, 1983).

Section Two
Friend 2 Friend Teaching Model

Fostering Mutual Friendships by Modeling, Labeling, Explaining and Normalizing

Friend 2 Friend programs follow a specifically designed teaching model for promoting understanding, acceptance and empathy by *modeling, labeling, explaining and normalizing the characteristics of autism.* Using age-appropriate tools, such as puppets and simulation games for younger children, each step in the teaching model is an essential part of the process of promoting mutual friendships between children on the autism spectrum and their typically developing peers.

Modeling
Friend 2 Friend programs support children in understanding puzzling social, communicative and self-regulating behaviors that they may see their peer or classmate on the autism spectrum exhibit. The first step in helping children understand the characteristics of autism is to provide a *visual model*. Modeling the characteristics of autism helps children form a plan or design of autism in their minds, which then becomes the basis for fostering understanding, acceptance and empathy with their peers on the autism spectrum.

Labeling
The next step in the teaching model is to support all children to accept the unusual social, communicative or self-regulating behaviors they may see their peer or classmate on the autism spectrum exhibit. After providing the visual model, we *label* the characteristics we have modeled. Labeling provides the children with a name for what they do not understand and helps them accept the characteristics or behaviors as genuine and real.

Explaining

Once the characteristics of autism have been modeled and labeled, we *explain* to children the sometimes puzzling social, communicative or self-regulating characteristics that they may see their peer or classmate on the autism spectrum exhibit. Explaining the meaning or purpose behind the characteristics helps children understand and accept their peer on the autism spectrum. Often typically developing children have difficulty understanding and accepting the unique characteristics of autism because the child with autism "looks normal," making them conclude that he is "choosing" to behave in a manner that is unusual rather than that the behaviors are symptoms of the autistic condition. Explaining the characteristics of autism provides children with the answers to the question, "Why does my friend do that?"

Normalizing

The final and most significant step in the Friend 2 Friend teaching model is to support children in empathizing with their peer on the autism spectrum. Once we have modeled and labeled the characteristics of autism and explained their purpose, we link the puzzling characteristics with common characteristics that all children exhibit. Such normalizing of the characteristics of autism provides children with an opportunity for emotional perspective taking, which allows them to truly walk in the shoes of the child with autism. Identifying with children on the autism spectrum shifts typically developing peers past simply understanding and accepting to feelings of empathy. These feelings of empathy facilitate prosocial behaviors, which form the basis for fostering mutual friendships between children on the autism spectrum and their typically developing peers, siblings and classmates (Eisenberg & Miller, 1987).

In short, each step in the Friend 2 Friend teaching model fosters understanding, acceptance and empathy by modeling, labeling, explaining and normalizing the characteristics of autism while never singling out the child with autism. It provides all children with information about autism and common vocabulary for further discussions and learning.

Friend 2 Friend Learning Goals

Woven within the program are Friend 2 Friend's Five Key Learning Goals and Seven Basic Friendship Tips. These learning outcomes and prosocial communication strategies provide children with the tools necessary to be successful social partners with their peers, siblings or classmates on the autism spectrum.

The Friend 2 Friends program works to promote the underlining concept – *we are all different in our own way, being a good friend means accepting differences* – by introducing children to the Five Key Learning Goals.

Five Key Learning Goals

1. *Recognize and accept differences in themselves and others:* Help children gain an understanding that everyone is different by identifying their own affinities (strengths or gifts) and their own disabilities (challenges or weaknesses).

2. *Recognize individuals with autism and peers with different kinds of minds as valuable friends:* Help children recognize that even though the student with autism may seem different, he still has great abilities. Those abilities or gifts make the child on the autism spectrum a valuable friend.

3. *Recognize that it is important to ask questions and express feelings:* Help children understand that by asking questions or expressing their feelings, they are learning new things about themselves and others.

4. *Empathize with what it feels like to have autism and different kinds of minds:* Help children identify with all their peers by providing an understanding of what it feels like to have autism.

5. *Promote positive relationships with all peers:* Help children recognize the importance of friendships for all children.

Prosocial Communication Strategies

Included in the Friend 2 Friend program are the Seven Basic Friendship Tips, which include prosocial communication strategies for enhancing social interactions between children on the autism spectrum and their peers. Increasing the prosocial behaviors (acts to help others, particularly when they have no goal other than to help) of typically developing peers is a key component. Studies show that when typically developing peers are trained in "how to" interact with their peers on the autism spectrum, appropriate social interactions increase significantly, and these skills generalize to new classrooms and students (Koegel & Schreibman, 1977; Koegel, O'Dell, & Koegel, 1987).

Seven Basic Friendship Tips

1. ***Get your friend's attention*** – Move closer and say your friend's name before you start to speak.

2. ***Use small sentences and gestures, and wait*** – Use small sentences and gestures – like pointing – to help your friend understand you. Then wait to give your friend time to answer you.

3. ***Watch your friend*** – Watch your friend to learn the things he or she likes to do.

4. ***Give your friend choices*** – When asking your friend to play, give your friend choices among the things you know he or she likes to do.

5. ***Ask your friend to talk*** – Ask you friend questions like, "What do you like to play or do?"

6. ***Use friendly words*** – When speaking to your friend, use words like "good job" or "give me five."

7. ***Accept differences*** – Everybody is different in his or her own way. Being a good friend means accepting differences.

Section Three
That's What's Different About Me! Puppet Program

Program Overview

That's What's Different About Me! program offers a meaningful way of introducing children to the concept of autism and related social communication disorders, while providing tools and strategies for interacting successfully with all peers. One of the goals of this program is to establish an inclusive classroom culture by promoting understanding, acceptance and empathy between children on the autism spectrum and their peers.

In an effort to provide information about autism in an age-appropriate manner, the *That's What's Different About Me!* program uses several learning opportunities to optimize learning for children with different learning styles or strengths. These learning opportunities include the following.

Introduction (Assigned Observer)
The introduction is designed to familiarize children with the *That's What's Different About Me!* program as well as provide an overview of each lesson. Begin each lesson by reviewing the steps in the lesson using the picture communication symbols (PCS) supplied in the resource materials section of this manual (see page 30). During each introduction, assign the children a job. By assigning the children a role during the teaching (assigned observer), you are increasing their buy-in to what they will be learning.

Puppet Play – DVD (Visual Learning Opportunity/Visual Model)

This interactive DVD includes a 10-minute video presentation of the *That's What's Different About Me!* puppet play. The video is designed to be played to a group or class of children who have direct or indirect contact with a child with autism spectrum or related social communication disorders. The puppet play provides children with a model of real-life situations by offering puppets representing a child with autism, typical peers, a teacher and a special education assistant. This visual model familiarizes children with the Five Key Learning Goals and the Seven Basic Friendship Tips, and explains characteristics of autism such as self-regulating behaviors, unusual social or communication styles, as well as student-directed teaching/learning techniques (typical peers teaching other peers how to interact with the child on the autism spectrum). The puppet play offers a viewpoint or perspective that all participants can relate to, including students and teachers, and introduces a common language for further discussion and learning.

"What Did Crystal Learn?" – DVD (Auditory and Visual Learning Opportunity)

"What Did Crystal Learn?" is an auditory and visual review of the learning goals and friendship tips presented in the puppet play and story book. Directly following the puppet play or book, the teacher reviews the Five Key Learning Goals and the Seven Basic Friendship Tips with the children using the PCS found in the resource section. This review offers a chance for children who are auditory and visual learners to gain additional insight into the program goals and tips, and teachers have an opportunity to evaluate which of the learning goals or friendship tips need to be emphasized in coming lessons or activities. You may choose to use the prerecorded "What Did Crystal Learn?" selection on the DVD or review the materials yourself. Provided below is a list of questions asked during the "What Did Crystal Learn?" review.

Key Questions for "What Did Crystal Learn?" Review

(Depending on the age of the children, you may wish to begin the review by asking, "What did Crystal learn?" This open-ended question often prompts the children to start generating ideas right away.)

Q: What did Crystal learn?

A: To be patient and understanding; that everyone has a different kind of mind; that we all have stims; we all want friends; the Seven Basic Friendship Tips, etc.

Q: Crystal learned "friendship tips" for playing with Freddie. What are some of the tips that Crystal learned?

A: Use the Seven Basic Friendship Tips board found on page 31 as a visual reminder for children.

Q: Did anyone hear the word "stim"? What was Crystal's stim, what was Angela's stim, what was Freddie's stim?

A: Finger sucking, nose picking, hair twirling, etc.

> Q: Did you know that everybody has stims? This is my stim (show the children hair twirling). Does anybody have this stim (use examples of common stims such as nail biting, hair twirling, shirt chewing and ask the children to raise their hands as their stim is called)?
> A: Children participate by raising their hand, and perhaps offer other examples of self-regulating behaviors.
> Q: Do you remember how Angela explained why we do stims?
> A: To concentrate, calm down or sometimes to stay awake.
> Q: Do you think Freddie has a different kind of mind?
> A: Everyone has a different mind.
> Q: What is Freddie good at?
> A: Drawing, computers.
> Q: What is Freddie not very good at?
> A: Making friends, talking.
> Q: What is Crystal good at?
> A: Dancing.
> Q: What is Crystal not very good at?
> A: Math.
> *Depending on the age of the children, this conversation may include having everyone raise their hands or talk about what they are good at and not good at.*
> Q: What was the most important thing that Crystal learned?
> A: Everybody wants friends.
> Q: Do you think Freddie wants friends? Do you think it might be hard for Freddie to make friends sometimes?
> A: If you know someone with Freddie's kind of mind, then think of the Seven Basic Friendship Tips and practice with your friend and each other every day.

Children's Story and Coloring Book (Auditory, Visual and Tactile Learning Opportunity)
This story and coloring book is an adaptation of the *That's What's Different About Me!* puppet play (as seen on the DVD). The book may be read to or by children as another means of generalizing the learning goals and friendship tips presented in the puppet play.

Follow-Up Activities (Tactile Learning Opportunity)
Located in the resource and materials section of this manual, you will find creative activities such as art projects and children's story books and games. These follow-up activities are a means for supporting the continued learning of the goals and tips introduced in the *That's What's Different About Me!* program. Many of these multisensory activities are designed to engage students who learn best by participating in hands-on activities.

Pass-the-Puppet Circle/Role-Playing Exercise (Tactile/Play Learning Opportunity)
This tactile learning opportunity provides children a chance to become the puppeteers. Working in smaller groups, children generalize the learning goals and friendship tips introduced in the puppet

play and story book and reviewed in the "What Did Crystal Learn?" portion of the program. You may choose to purchase puppets, ask the children to bring puppets from home or make puppets for/or with the children.

Supporting the Focus Child's Participation

All children, including those on the autism spectrum, need information about autism to achieve a shared understanding and common language, which is the basis for fostering mutual friendships. *That's What's Different About Me!* program is designed for the full participation of all children, including the focus child with autism. However, some children may need extra support to participate. Listed below are some suggestions for supporting the full participation of the focus child in group activities and lessons.

Communication

Many individuals on the autism spectrum have receptive and expressive communication differences. Even the most verbal child may not always understand what he or she is hearing or may struggle with sharing thoughts and ideas. Using visual teaching strategies such as pictures, picture communication symbols, sign language, gestures and the written word helps students participate with their peers in classroom activities (Beukelman & Mirenda, 1998). In the resources section of this manual, you will find visual supports as seen in the *That's What's Different About Me!* DVD and book. We suggest you make up a Seven Basic Friendship Tips picture communication symbols board (see pages 29-31) for supporting all children with visual learning strengths participating in this program.

Pre-Teach or Prime

Many individuals on the autism spectrum have difficulty transitioning to new or different activities, projects or programs. In an effort to support these children to participate fully with their peers, we suggest pre-teaching or priming the focus child by introducing each lesson ahead of the group participation.

Below are some suggestions for how to pre-teach or prime the focus child:
- Have the child watch the puppet play video in a quiet and safe place (invite a peer)
- Send the puppet play video home with the focus child so he may share the learning opportunity with his family
- Read the children's story and coloring book in a quiet and safe place (invite a peer)
- Introduce the focus child to the puppets in a quiet, safe environment (invite a peer)
- Provide the focus child with the visual supports found in the resource section
- Rehearse the Seven Basic Friendship Tips using the visual supports (invite a peer)

Movement Differences

Many individuals with autism have movement differences such as impeded postures, uneven gait, excess movements, stuttering, and difficulties starting, stopping and switching movements. Understanding and recognizing movement differences can be helpful in supporting students to participate fully with their peers in this program. For example, the focus child may have difficulty sitting through the entire presentation. In this case, allow the child to hold one of the puppets or get up and move around the room. Sometimes it is a good idea to have the entire class take a stretch break.

Self-Regulation Differences

Many individuals with autism are more or less sensitive than typical in the areas of hearing, touch, smell, sight, taste, balance and movement. In an effort to regulate these sensory issues, many engage in self-regulating behaviors such as hand flapping, clapping, rocking, pacing and verbal sounds. These "stims" are the child's way of keeping herself at the right state of arousal. If the focus child needs to self-regulate during the program, please allow her to (Prizant, 2002). Everybody has stims, what are yours?

Friendship Differences

Many individuals with autism wish to have friends but lack the necessary social skills. We must be careful not to misinterpret a lack of skills as a lack of desire. Supporting children on the autism spectrum to fully participate as active members of their class is critical for fostering mutual friendships. Using pre-teaching or priming techniques and allowing for communication, social, movement and self-regulating differences creates a truly inclusive classroom/school culture. Further, these techniques support the full participation of children on the autism spectrum by helping them fit in, not stand out.

Implementing the Program

When implementing the program at home or at school, we suggest that the learning be divided over several sessions. On the following pages we have provided three lesson plans. Each lesson plan will provide children with visual, tactile and auditory learning opportunities.

Lesson Plan 1 – The Puppet Play

1. Introduction
2. Puppet Play DVD
3. "What Did Crystal Learn?" Review
4. Follow-Up Activity (see pages 24-25)

Objectives:
The children will ...
- Become familiar with the puppet play story
- Identify with the puppet characters
- Identify some of the Seven Basic Friendship Tips
- Identify some of the Five Key Learning Goals

Materials Required:
- Introduction – PCS (see page 30)
- Seven Basic Friendship Tips board – PCS (see pages 30-31)
- Follow-up activity materials (see pages 24-25 for suggested follow-up activities)

Time:
- 5-minute introduction
- 10-minute puppet play
- 5- to 10-minute "What Did Crystal Learn?" review
- 15-minute follow-up activity

Teaching the Lesson

Step 1: Introduction (Assigned Observer)
Using the PCS found on page 30, review the steps in the lesson plan with the children:

"We will watch the puppet play video" – Talk with the children about the puppet play video, including what they are about to see and the overall learning objective of the Friend 2 Friend programs (e.g., "This play is about friendships and how to be a good friend."). Ask the children to listen to what Crystal (a puppet in the play) is going to learn. (Assigned Observer)

"What Did Crystal Learn?" – Explain to the children that after the puppet play is over, you would like to talk to them about what Crystal learned.

"Then we will do an art project related to the puppet play" – Explain to the children that you will do an art project or other follow-up activity after you finish talking about what Crystal learned. (Suggestions for follow-up activities may be found on pages 24-25.)

Step 2: The Puppet Play (Model or Visual Learning Opportunity)
Play the DVD of the puppet play for the children. You may wish to preview the puppet play to skim for new vocabulary words to introduce. Remind the student to listen carefully to what Crystal is going to learn in the puppet play.

Step 3: "What Did Crystal Learn?" (Auditory Learning/Performance Feedback)
Review with the children the Five Key Learning Goals and Seven Basic Friendship Tips modeled in the puppet play, using the PCS.

Step 4: Follow-Up Activity
See suggestion for follow-up activities on pages 24-25.

Lesson Plan 2 – Children's Coloring Book

1. Introduction
2. *That's What's Different About Me! Children's Story and Coloring Book*
3. "What Did Crystal Learn?" Review
4. Follow-Up Activity (see pages 24-25 for suggestions on follow-up activities)

Objectives:
The children will …
- Identify with a puppet character from the puppet play
- Identify most of the Seven Basic Friendship Tips
- Read along with the story
- Investigate the concepts of the Five Key Learning Goals and Seven Basic Friendship Tips

Materials Required:
- Introduction – PCS (see page 30)
- Seven Basic Friendship Tips board – PCS (see pages 29-31)
- Follow-up activity materials (see pages 24-25 for suggestions on follow-up activities)
- Copies of the story and coloring book

Time:
- 5-minute review
- 10-minute book reading
- 5- to 10-minute "What Did Crystal Learn?" review
- 15-minute follow-up activity

Teaching the Lesson

Step 1: Introduction (Assigned Observer)
Using the PCS found on page 30, review the steps in the lesson plan with the children:

"We will read the *That's What's Different About Me!* story book" – Explain to the children that it is a story based on the puppet play that they saw in the previous lesson. Ask the children to pay close attention to Angela while reading through the book. (Assigned Observer)

"What Did Crystal Learn?" – Explain that you would like to review with them what Crystal learned after reading the book.

Art project – Explain to the children about the art project you have chosen as a follow-up activity.

Step 2: Read the children's story and coloring book. (Depending on the age of the children, you may wish to provide them with copies of the books so they can read along.)

Step 3: "What Did Crystal Learn?"
Review with the children the Five Key Learning Goals and Seven Basic Friendship Tips in the children's story book using the PCS found on pages 30-31.

Step 4: Follow-Up Activity
See suggestion for follow-up activities on pages 24-25.

Lesson Plan 3 – Puppet Role-Playing

1. Introduction
2. Puppet Play DVD
3. Pass-the-Puppets Circle/"What Did Crystal Learn?" Review (see instructions below)
4. Follow-Up Activity – Puppet Role-Playing (see instructions below)

Objectives:
The children will …
- Identify with a puppet character from the puppet play
- Identify the Seven Basic Friendship Tips
- Investigate the concepts of the Five Key Learning Goals
- Investigate the puppets and practice the Seven Basic Friendship Tips

Materials Required:
- Introduction – PCS (see pages 29-31)
- Seven Basic Friendship Tips board – PCS (see pages 30-31)
- 2 or more puppets and props

Time:
- 5-minute review
- 10-minute puppet play DVD
- 5- to 10-minute "What Did Crystal Learn?" review
- 15-minute Pass-the-Puppet Circle

Teaching the Lesson

Step 1: Introduction (Assigned Observer)
Using the PCS found on page 30, review the steps in the lesson plan with the children:
1. "We will watch the puppet play" – Ask the children to play close attention to Freddie.
2. "What Did Crystal Learn?"
3. "Pass-the-Puppet Circle" (see instructions below).
4. Puppet Role-Playing – Explain to the children how to do the puppet role-playing.

Step 2: The Puppet Play (Model or Visual Learning Opportunity)

Step 3: Pass-the-Puppet Circle (Free Exploration)
Have the children sit in a circle on the floor. Pass the puppet from child to child, ensuring each child gets a turn with the puppets. You will ask the children to pass the puppet to the friend on their right (you may use a bell or hand claps). This is an opportunity for free exploration with the puppets. While the children are sharing the puppets, you may wish to review the learning goals and friendship tips.

Step 4: Follow-Up Activity – Puppet Role-Playing
This role-playing lesson offers children a chance to become the puppeteers while practicing the Seven Basic Friendship Tips.
- Assign children to small groups (2-4 children per group).
- Assign each group one of the Seven Basic Friendship Tips. Ask the children to review the tips and take turns using the puppets to act out the tips.
- Set a time limit for the groups to practice their assigned tip.
- Model with one of the children how to role-play a friendship tip using the puppets.
- When the allotted time is up, ask the children if they are ready to perform their tip for the class. If some children do not want to perform, allow them to sit out.

Materials and Props for Follow-Up Activity – Puppet Role-Play
This follow-up activity may require a few extra puppets and materials. We suggest having enough puppets for the children to practice their friendship tip. Ask the children to bring a puppet from home, purchase puppets or make puppets with or for the children as one of the follow-up activities. You will also need a table and chairs as a stage for the puppets and some props such as small toys or games. You may choose to make props such as the computer or purchase a travel *Trouble* game as seen in the puppet play. Other options include making the props as a follow-up activity or asking the children to bring some of their favorite toys and games from home.

Follow-Up Activities and Resources

Follow-Up Projects and Activities

Seven Basic Friendship Tips Art Project: Post the Seven Basic Friendship Tips on the wall in the classroom. As an art project, ask each student to pick his or her favorite tip and draw, paint, etc., a picture to illustrate it. Provide time for the children to share their finished art with the class, and then display the pictures in the hallways throughout the school for the entire student body to see.

That's What's Different About Me! Children's Story and Coloring Book: Assign children to pairs; ask each pair to choose their favorite page from the book. Then ask them to color, draw or make a poster of their favorite friendship tip. Once the project is completed, the children may be asked to read and show their project to the rest of the class.

Seven Basic Friendship Tips Puppet Show: Put on a puppet show. Have the children write and produce a brief puppet play about friendships, including the focus child. Teach the children the steps for producing a puppet play and assign roles and responsibilities. Each step in preparing for the puppet show can act as a follow-up activity to build on the children's learning of the concept and tips modeled in the puppet play. The steps (follow-up activities) in creating a puppet play might include script writing, making props, creating scenery, making or purchasing puppets, practicing the play and finally putting on the puppet show. The children may perform the show for other classes to support other students learning the Friend 2 Friend learning goals and friendship tips.

Finger Print Art: Have the children create a self-portrait by using ink pads and the children's fingers to produce the drawings. Discuss how each person is unique just like our finger prints are unique and different.

Seven Basic Friendship Tips Classroom List: Focus students on creating a classroom where everyone feels accepted and belongs. As a class project, generate a class friendship tips list of rules. To encourage participation put the children into smaller groups to brainstorm ideas, then vote on which ideas to include on your class friendship tip list. Once the list is completed, have the children work cooperatively to create a poster for the classroom or school.

Social Clubs: Have a small group of children create a social club designed around the focus child's special interests or skills. Suggestions include Thomas the Tank Engine club, a video club, an art club, a Lego club. These clubs meet twice a week for 20-30 minutes at lunch time. Have the peers come up with ideas for how to include their friends with different kinds of minds.

Other Great Ideas

Signing Sally: After the Friend 2 Friend puppet presentation visited a local preschool, the teacher purchased a puppet identical to our "Sherry" puppet and called her Sally. Once a week this teacher teaches the children in the 3- and 4-year-old classes sign language in an effort to help the child with autism make connection with his peers.

Puppet Journals: Students in Richmond, British Columbia, wrote in their journals about their experiences during the Friend 2 Friend program and what they had learned about autism and about themselves. The principal of the school was so impressed by the journals that she wrote her own journal about what she had learned about autism. The journals were posted in the hallway to share with the entire student body.

Discussion Time: Students in Delta, British Columbia, returned to their classroom after a Friend 2 Friend presentation and began discussing "self-regulating behaviors." The teacher reported that the class had lively discussions about "stims" and many of the other things they had learned during the presentation. She also reported that for first time the focus student (with autism) participated fully in the discussion along with the other students as "an equal."

Selected Books for Children

Bleach, F. (2001). *Everybody is different – A book for young people who have brothers or sisters with autism.* Shawnee Mission, KS: Autism Asperger Publishing Company.

Bishop, B. (2002). *My friend with autism.* Arlington, TX: Future Horizons.

Brown, L. K., & Brown, M. (1998). *How to be a friend.* New York: Little, Brown and Company.

Buron, K. D. (2006). *When my worries get too big!* Shawnee Mission, KS: Autism Asperger Publishing Company.

Edwards, A. (2001). *Taking autism to school.* Plainview, NY: JayJo Books, LLC.

Ely, L., & Dunbar, P. (2004). *Looking after Louise.* Morton Grove, IL: Albert Whitman & Company.

Gagnon, E., & Myles, B. S. (1999). *This is Asperger Syndrome.* Shawnee Mission, KS: Autism Asperger Publishing Company.

Henkes, K. (1991). *Chrysanthemum.* New York: Greenwillow Books.

Larson, E. M. (2006). *I am utterly unique.* Shawnee Mission, KS: Autism Asperger Publishing Company.

Lesada, J., & Lancelle, M. (2006). *Sundays with Matthew.* Shawnee Mission, KS: Autism Asperger Publishing Company.

Lester, H. (1988). *Tacky the Penguin.* Boston: Houghton Mifflin Company.

Levine, M. (2002). *All kinds of minds.* Cambridge, MA: Educational Publishing Service.

Lowell, J., & Tuchel, T. (2005). *My best friend Will.* Shawnee Mission, KS: Autism Asperger Publishing Company.

Murrell, D. (2001). *Tobin learns to make friends.* Arlington, TX: Future Horizons.

Murrell, D. (2004). *Oliver Onion.* Shawnee Mission, KS: Autism Asperger Publishing Company.

Parr, T. (2001). *It's okay to be different.* New York: Little, Brown and Company.

Peralta, S. (2002). *All about my brother.* Shawnee Mission, KS: Autism Asperger Publishing Company.

Other Resources – Books for Parents and Professionals

Agran, M., King-Sears, M., Wehmeyer, M., & Copeland, S. (2003). *Teachers' guide to inclusive practices, student directed learning*. Baltimore: Brookes Publishing.

Attwood, T. (1998). *Asperger's syndrome: A guide for parents and professionals*. Philadelphia: Jessica Kingsley.

Attwood, T. (2002). Profile of friendship skills in asperger's syndrome. *The Jenison Autism Journal*, 14-3, 2-7. Jenison School Publications.

Baron-Cohen, S. (1995). *Mindblindness: An essay on autism and theory of mind*. Cambridge, MA: MIT Press.

Bauminger, N., & Kasari, C. (2000). Loneliness and friendship in high-functioning children with autism. *Child Development, 71,* 447-456.

Burkowski, W. M., Newcomb, A. F., & Hartup, W. W. (Eds.). (1996). *The company they keep: Friendship in childhood and adolescence*. Cambridge: Cambridge University Press.

Cotton, K. (1992). *Developing empathy in children and youth* (Close-Up #13). Portland, OR: Northwest Regional Education Laboratory.

Coucouvanis, J. (2001). *Super Skills – A social skills group program for children with Asperger Syndrome, high-functioning autism and related challenges*. Shawnee Mission, KS: Autism Asperger Publishing Company.

Dunn Buron, K., & Curtis, M. (2003). *The incredible 5-point scale*. Shawnee Mission, KS: Autism Asperger Publishing Company.

Dunn, M. (2005). *Social skills in our schools: A social skills program for verbal children with pervasive developmental disorders and their typical peers*. Shawnee Mission, KS: Autism Asperger Publishing Company.

Duke, M., Nowicki, S., & Martin E, (1996). *Teaching your child the language of social success*, Atlanta, GA: Peachtree Publishers Ltd.

Gray, C. (2002). The sixth sense II. *The Morning News*, 14, 1 & 2, 1-17. Jenison, MI: Jenison Public Schools.

Gray, C. (2001). *Taming the recess jungle: Socially simplifying recess for students with autism and related disorders*. Jenison, MI: Jenison Public Schools.

Kluth, P. (2003). *You're going to love this kid*. Baltimore: Brookes Publishing.

Levine, M. (2001). *Educational care: A system for understanding and helping children with learning problems at home and in school*. Cambridge, MA: Educational Publishing Service.

Manolson, A. (1992). *It takes two to talk: A parent's guide to help children communicate*. Toronto, Ontario, Canada: Hanen Centre Publications.

Meyer, L. H., Park, H. S., Grenot-Scheyer, M., Schwarts, S., & Harry, B. (1998). *Making friends: The influences of culture and development*. Baltimore: Paul H. Brookes Publishing Co.

Moyes, R. (2001). *Incorporating social goals in the classroom*. London: Jessica Kingsley Publishers.

Myles, B., & Schelvan, R. (2003). *The hidden curriculum*. Shawnee Mission, KS: Autism Asperger Publishing Company.

Myles, B. S., & Simpson, R. L. (1998). *Asperger syndrome: A guide for educators and practitioners*. Austin, TX: PRO-ED.

Staub, D. (1998). *Delicate threads – Friendships between children with and without special needs in inclusive settings*. Bethesda, MD: Woodbine House.

Sussman, F. (2002). *More than words*. Toronto, Ontario, Canada: Hanen Centre Publications.

Thompson, A., & Rubin, K (2002). *The friendship factor: Helping our children navigate their social world why it matters for their success*. New York: Penguin Books.

Wagner, S. (1998). *Inclusive programming for elementary students with autism*. Fort Worth, TX: Future Horizons.

Wolfberg, P. J. (1999). *Play and imagination in children with autism*. New York: Teachers College Press, Columbia University.

Wolfberg, P. J. (2003). *Peer play and the autism spectrum: The art of guiding children's socialization and imagination*. Shawnee, KS: Autism Asperger Publishing Company.

Friend 2 Friend Materials – Augmentative Communication Board/Friendship Poster

Materials You Will Need ...
- Thick poster board
- Velcro
- Laminator
- PCS (see pages 30-31)

Instructions
To make the Friend 2 Friend augmentative communication board use a large thick poster board or magnet board. Print enlarged versions of the PCS and laminate them. Then attach Velcro to the back of each. Put the opposite side of the Velcro on the poster board. When reviewing the Seven Basic Friendship Tips with the children, use the PCS to support learning by placing them on the board as a clue to help the children remember or after the children have told you each tip. Also post a copy of the Seven Basic Friendship Tips poster in the classroom so it may be reviewed as needed.

Introduction PCS

Puppet play	"What Did Crystal Learn?"	Pass-the-puppet circle
Art project	Read book	Puppet role-playing

The Picture Communication Symbols, used with permission from Mayer-Johnson Inc., PO Box 1579, Solana Beach, CA 92075, 800 588 4548 (phone) URL www.mayer-johnson.com

Seven Basic Friendship Tips PCS

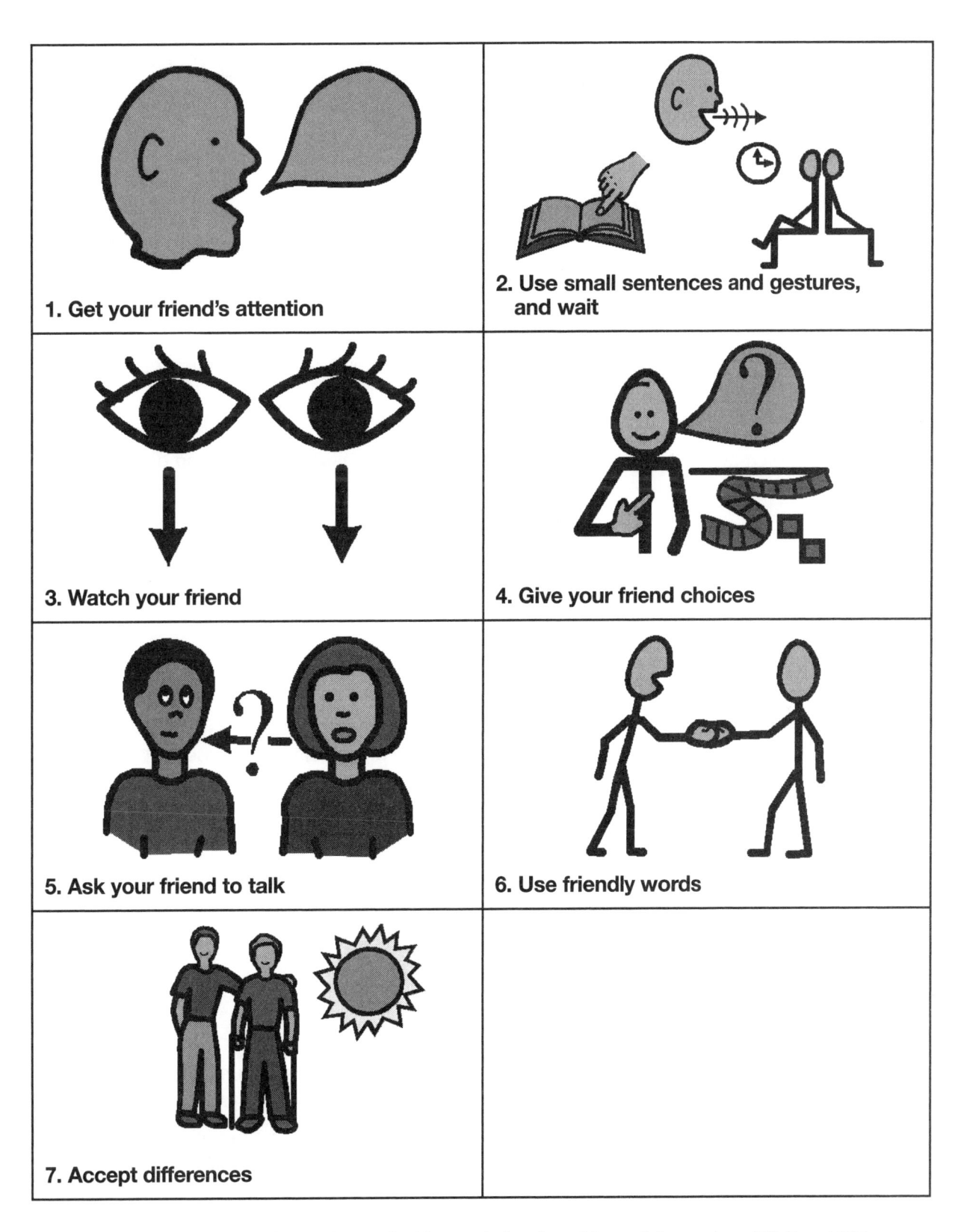

1. Get your friend's attention	2. Use small sentences and gestures, and wait
3. Watch your friend	4. Give your friend choices
5. Ask your friend to talk	6. Use friendly words
7. Accept differences	

The Picture Communication Symbols, used with permission from Mayer-Johnson Inc., PO Box 1579, Solana Beach, CA 92075, 800 588 4548 (phone) URL www.mayer-johnson.com

Section Four
Regular and Continuous Support

The *That's What's Different About Me!* puppet program offers a first step towards fostering mutual friendship between children with autism and their typically developing peers. However, the path to mutual friendships requires regular and continuous support to be successful.

Friend 2 Friend's sister model, the Integrated Play Groups (IPG), is designed to support children on the autism spectrum to enhance play and friendship by focusing on supporting peers to understand how to play with the children on the spectrum.

In this section the creator of the IPG model, Dr. Pamela Wolfberg, offers readers an overview of the IPG model.

Integrated Play Groups (IPG) Model

Dr. Pamela Wolfberg

Like the Friend 2 Friend model, the Integrated Play Groups (IPG) model was created out of deep concern for the many children on the autism spectrum who are missing out on peer play and friendships as vital childhood experiences (for detailed descriptions, see Wolfberg, 1999, 2003). Defining features of autism include a lack of varied and imaginative or imitative play and a failure to develop peer relationships appropriate to developmental level. These difficulties are closely connected to characteristic impairments in the development of reciprocal social interaction, communication and imagination (American Psychiatric Association, 2000). Guided by current theory, research and evidence-based practices, the IPG model reflects a blending of approaches to foster development in each of these areas.

The IPG model is designed to support children of diverse ages and abilities on the autism spectrum (*novice players*) in mutually enjoyed play experiences with typical peers/siblings (*expert players*) within school, home and community settings. Small groups of children regularly play together under the guidance of an adult facilitator (*play guide*) within specially designed environments. Through a carefully tailored system of support, emphasis is placed on maximizing children's developmental potential as well as intrinsic desire to play, socialize and form meaningful relationships with peers. Of equal importance is teaching peers to be empathetic, responsive and accepting of children's differing social, communication and play styles. A further intent is for children to mediate their own play activities with minimal adult guidance.

Based on award-winning research, the IPG model has been adopted by numerous schools and programs at the local, national and international level, and is becoming widely recognized as among best practices for children with autism. Positive outcomes for children have been demonstrated through a series of studies carried out by and replicating the work of Wolfberg and colleagues (see publications in www.autisminstitute.com). Advances in reciprocal social interaction, communication, language, representational play and related symbolic activity (writing and drawing) were noted for the children with autism, while increases in self-esteem, awareness, empathy and acceptance of individual differences were noted for the typical peers. Generalization and social validation were also documented as children carried over skills and formed mutual friendships that extended beyond the IPG setting. For more information, please refer to the following Fact Sheet on Integrated Play Groups and Features of the Integrated Play Groups Model.

The child shall have full opportunity for play and recreation, which should be directed to the same purpose as education; society and public authorities shall endeavor to promote the employment of this right ... United Nations Declaration of Human Rights, 1948, Principle 7

Fact Sheet on Integrated Play Groups (IPG)

What are Integrated Play Groups?
The IPG model was created by Pamela Wolfberg, Ph.D. (San Francisco State University and Autism Institute on Peer Relations and Play), to address the unique and complex challenges children on the autism spectrum experience in peer relations and play. Integrated Play Groups consist of small groups of children on the autism spectrum (novice players) and typical peers/siblings (expert players) who regularly play together under the guidance of a qualified adult facilitator (play guide).

What is the purpose of Integrated Play Groups?
Research shows that peer play experiences are a vital part of children's learning, development and culture. Children on the autism spectrum face many obstacles playing and socializing with peers. Integrated Play Groups are designed to enhance children's social interaction, communication, play and imagination. An equally important focus is on teaching the peer group to be more accepting, responsive and inclusive of children who relate and play in different ways.

Who may participate in Integrated Play Groups?
Integrated Play Groups are customized as a part of a child's individual education/therapy program. The IPG model is appropriate for preschool – elementary-aged children (3 to 11 years). Play

groups are made up of 3 to 5 children, with a higher ratio of expert to novice players. Novice players include children of all abilities on the autism spectrum and with related special needs. Expert players include typical peers/siblings with strong social, communication and play skills.

Where and when do Integrated Play Groups take place?
Integrated Play Groups take place in natural play environments within school, home, therapy or community settings. Play groups generally meet twice a week for 30- to 60-minute sessions over a 6- to 12-month period. Sessions are carried out in specially designed play spaces that include a wide range of motivating materials and activities.

How do Integrated Play Groups work?
Play sessions are tailored to the children's unique interests, abilities and needs. The adult methodically guides novice and expert players to engage in mutually enjoyed play activities that encourage reciprocal social interaction, communication and imagination – such as pretending, constructing, art, music, movement and interactive games. Gradually the children learn how to play together with less and less adult support.

What are the benefits of Integrated Play Groups?
As demonstrated through award-winning research, novice players have benefited in the areas of social interaction, communication, language, representational play and related symbolic activity (writing and drawing). Expert players have benefited by showing greater self-esteem, awareness, empathy and acceptance of individual differences. Both novice and expert players have formed mutual friendships while having fun together.

For more information
Autism Institute on Peer Relations and Play – Center for Integrated Play Groups
website: www.autisminstitute.com or www.wolfberg.com
E-mail: pamela@wolfberg.com

Features of the Integrated Play Groups (IPG) Model

Mission
To provide a haven for children with diverse abilities to create genuine play worlds together, where they may reach their social and imaginative potential, as well as have fun and make friends.

IPG Program Design

Objectives
- Foster spontaneous, mutually enjoyed, reciprocal play with peers
- Expand/diversify social and symbolic play repertoire
- Enhance peer-mediated play activities with minimal adult guidance

Service Delivery
- Preschool – elementary-aged children (3 to 11 years)
- Customized as part of education/therapy program
- Led by trained adult facilitator (play guide)

Play Group Composition
3 to 5 children per group – higher ratio of expert to novice players
- Novice players – children of all abilities on the autism spectrum and with related special needs
- Expert players – typically developing peers/siblings

IPG Environmental Design

Schedule
Play group sessions meet 2 times per week for 30-60 minutes over 6- to 12-month period

Play Setting
- Natural integrated settings – school, home, therapy or community
- Specially designed play spaces – wide range of motivating materials, activities and themes encourage interactive and imaginative play

Play Session Structure
Consistent routines, rituals and visual supports foster familiarity, predictability and a cohesive group identity

IPG Assessment

Observation Framework

Naturalistic observation of children at play:
- Social play styles
- Symbolic dimensions of play
- Social dimensions of play
- Communicative functions and means
- Play preferences – diversity of play

Assessment Tools
- Play Questionnaire
- Play Preference Inventory
- Integrated Play Groups Observation
- Profile of Individual Play Development
- Record of Monthly Progress in IPG (with sample goals)
- IPG Summative Report

IPG Intervention

Guided Participation

System of support to facilitate social interaction, communication, play and imagination by skillfully applying the following practices:
- Monitoring play initiations
- Scaffolding play
- Social-communication guidance
- Play guidance

American Psychiatric Association. (2000). *Diagnostic and statistical manual of mental disorders – IV*. Washington, DC: Author.

Wolfberg, P. J. (1999). *Play and imagination in children with autism*, New York: Teachers College Press, Columbia University. http://www.wolfberg.com/Publications.htm

Wolfberg, P. J. (2003). *Peer play and the autism spectrum: The art of guiding children's socialization and imagination*. Shawnee Mission, KS: Autism Asperger Publishing Company.

References

Asher, S. R., Hymel, S., & Remshaw, P. D. (1984). Loneliness in children. *Child Development, 55,* 1456-1464.

Berndt, T. J. (1999). Friends' influence on students' adjustment to school. *Educational Psychologist, 34,* 15-28.

Berndt, T. J. (2002). Friendship quality and social development. *Current Directions in Psychological Science, 11,* 7-10.

Beukelman, D., & Mirenda, P. (1998). *Augmentative and alternative communication, 2nd ed.* Baltimore: Paul H. Brookes.

Eisenberg, N., & Miller, P. A. (1987). Empathy and prosocial behavior. *Psychological Bulletin, 101,* 91-119.

Feshbach, N. D., & Feshbach, S. (1983). *Learning to care: Classroom activities for social and affective development.* Glenview, IL: Scott, Foresman.

Hartup, W. W. (1989). Social relationships and their developmental significance. *American Psychologist, 44,* 120-126.

Hartup, W. W. (1991). Having friends, making and keeping friends: Relationships as education contexts. *Early Report, 19,* 1-4.

Kluth, P. (2003). *You're going to love this kid.* Baltimore: Brookes Publishing.

Koegel, R. L., O'Dell, M. C., & Koegel, L. K. (1987). A natural language teaching paradigm for non-verbal autistic children. *Journal of Autism and Developmental Disorders, 17,* 187-200.

Koegel, R. L., & Schreibman, L. (1977). Teaching autistic children to respond to simultaneous multiple cues. *Journal of Experimental Child Psychology, 24,* 299-311.

Ladd, G. W. (1990). Having friends, Keeping friends, making friends, and being liked by peers in the classroom: Predictors of children's early school adjustment? *Child Development, 61,* 1081-1100.

Levine, M. (2001). *Educational care: A system for understanding and helping children with learning problems at home and in school.* Cambridge, MA: Educational Publishing Service.

Mayer-Johnson. (2002). *Writing with symbols.* Solana Beach, CA: Author. http://www.mayer-johnson.com.

McCracken, H. (2004). *Enhancing peer relations in children with ASD: Friend 2 Friend model.* Paper presented at the BC Association of Speech-Language Pathologists and Audiologists (BCASLPA), Kelowna, BC, Canada.

McCracken, H. (2005a). Friend 2 Friend: Fostering mutual friendships for children with ASD. *Autism-Asperger Digest*, Jan-Feb, 6-15.

McCracken, H. (2005b). Friend 2 Friend programs help children with autism feel safe to say, "I'm autistic too." *Autism Spectrum Quarterly, 2,* 13.

McCracken, H. (2005c). *Fostering mutual friendships for children with ASD - The Friend 2 Friend model*. Paper presented to the Autism Society of America National Conference, Nashville, TN.

Prizant, B. (2002). *Secrets model*. Richmond School District Professional Day Conference, Richmond, BC, Canada.

Thompson, A., & Rubin, K. (2002). *The friendship factor: Helping our children navigate their social world – Why it matters for their success*. New York: Penguin Putnam Inc.

Wing, L. (1981). Asperger's syndrome: A clinical account. *Psychological Medicine, 11,* 115-129.

Wolfberg, P., McCracken, H., & Tuchel, T. (in press). Guiding children with ASD in peer relations and play in inclusive educational settings. In K. Dunn Buron & P. J. Wolfberg (Eds.), *Educating children on the autism spectrum: Translating theory into meaningful practice*. Shawnee Mission, KS: Autism Asperger Publishing Company.